Eric Plants a Garden

Eric Plants a Garden

Story and Photographs by **JEAN HUDLOW**

ALBERT WHITMAN & Company · Chicago

Standard Book Number 8075-2136-1.
Library of Congress Card Number 79-150803.
©Copyright 1971 by Jean Hudlow.
Published simultaneously in Canada by George J. McLeod, Limited, Toronto.
All rights reserved. Printed in the United States of America.

A Garden of Your Own

You can grow a big garden of your own, like Eric's, or you can plant vegetables in a corner of your yard, a wooden tub, or flowerpots along a path. You can plant rows of lettuce and radishes around a flower bed or in a kitchen planter. Maybe you can plant a garden at school.

Eric found vegetables need sun, water, soil, and room to grow. Plant your garden where sun shines on it all day. Rain may keep your garden wet, or you can water it with a hose, as Eric does. Vegetables grow in all kinds of soil. It helps to add fertilizer or soil conditioner because plants grow better.

Plants need enough room to grow. Eric planted many radishes in a small space and picked them in four weeks. His pumpkins needed a lot of room and four months to grow. Seed packages tell when to plant seeds, how deep, how far apart rows should be, and how to thin and water vegetables.

Spring vegetables besides those Eric planted are beans, squash, cucumbers, melons, and tomatoes. If you live where it doesn't snow, plant peas, cabbages, onions, and lettuce in late summer.

Birds, insects, and worms may visit your garden. They are fascinating to watch. Butterflies, ladybugs, and earthworms help your garden grow. Pests like snails and caterpillars nibble at vegetables. Pick them off and put them out of your garden.

For more help in growing your garden, talk to other gardeners, a nurseryman, or your county agricultural extension agent. You can get helpful booklets from the U.S. Department of Agriculture in Washington, D.C.

Even in winter when it rains and snows, it is fun to look at seed catalogs and plan your garden for spring.

It is a bright spring day
full of sunshine and butterflies—
and Eric wants something new to do.

"What can I do?" he asks.
"Fly a kite?   There's no wind.
Play baseball? My bat is broken."

Eric thinks and thinks.
Then he has a great idea.

"I'll plant a garden!" Eric says.
"Let's see. I'll have lettuce and radishes
and carrots and onions.
And how about corn and maybe pumpkins?

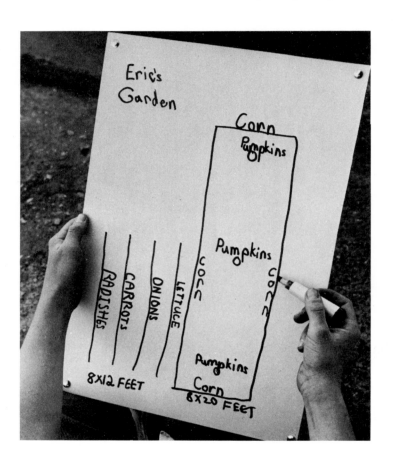

First, I'll draw a plan for my garden."

Plants grow from seeds.
So Eric goes to the store to buy seeds for his garden.
He sees many kinds of seeds—it's hard to know what to buy.
But at last Eric finds the ones he wants.
He pays for the seeds and goes home.

Eric finds the best place for his garden.
It's back of his house.
But look at all those weeds!

Eric pulls weeds,

and hoes weeds

and rakes weeds.

Now Eric is ready
to make his garden.
He turns over the
earth with his spade.

He breaks up
the chunks of dirt
with his hoe

and smooths the dirt
with his rake.

The ground needs a big drink of water so the soil will be wet way, way down.

Eric needs a drink, too.

Next day Eric tests the soil.
Is it ready for planting?
Not too wet. Not too dry. No big lumps.
The dirt crumbles into little pieces.
It is just right!

Eric gets some fertilizer
for his garden.
Fertilizer is plant food.
Plants take up this
food through their roots.
This helps the plants
grow big and strong.

Eric sprinkles fertilizer on his garden.
He rakes it into the soil.
Now he's ready to plant the seeds.

Eric gets his seeds.
It's time to plant them.
In one garden plot, Eric is going
to plant lettuce, carrot, radish,
and onion seeds.

He makes rows 12 inches apart.
He uses a ruler to make sure
his rows are far enough apart.
Then he makes the rows with a pole.

Eric tears a corner off
the package of carrot seeds.
He shakes some seeds out
into his hand.

Will these tiny seeds
really grow into carrots?

The best fun of all is planting the seeds! "Not too deep," Eric says.

He covers the seeds with earth and sprinkles the garden with water.

Eric knows an easy way to show
what he's planted in each row.

Eric wants to grow some giant pumpkins, so he plants them this way.

He digs a hole 4 inches deep. He puts a scoop of fertilizer in the hole.

He covers the hole with dirt.
Then he pokes 4 little holes, 1 inch deep.

Eric plants a pumpkin seed in each little hole.

Eric's mother gives him a surprise—
some onion sets.

"They look like baby onions," Eric thinks.
He knows they grow faster than onion seeds.

Eric plants his onion sets
12 inches apart.

"One more thing to plant," Eric says.
"And it's best of all."

Corn!
Nothing tastes as good as corn on the cob.

Even the seeds look good enough to eat.

Eric makes a row
around the big garden plot.
He plants the corn.

Corn needs a lot
of room to grow.
Eric drops the seeds
about 6 inches apart.

Eric makes sure his garden gets enough water.
When it does not rain,
he waters his vegetables with a hose.

One day Eric sees some little green sprouts—

The radishes are up!

Then the carrots come up.

And the onions come up.

When the plants are about 2 inches high,
Eric thins them.
He pulls out some of the plants.
Then the ones left have room to grow.

One day Eric finds that birds have pulled up
some of the corn sprouts.

But Eric knows what to do.
He ties pieces of cloth on strings
all around the corn.

When the wind
moves the cloth,
the birds fly away.
Shoo!

To water his corn,
Eric digs a ditch near
the cornstalks.

Water runs down the ditch
and soaks into the ground
where the roots are.

Eric thins his corn plants
to make them 12 inches apart.

He uses his hoe to get
rid of the weeds.
Charlie Cat wants to help.

The radishes,

the lettuce,
and the onions
are ready to pick.

HAPPY DAY!

"Let's see. I'll have lettuce and radishes and onions!" Eric says.

"There is nothing like a salad from your own garden."

Are the carrots ready to pick?
There is one way to find out.

Pull one up,

wash it off—

—and eat it!

Corn starts small

and grows taller

and taller

and TALLER.

The tall corn plants
have tassels at the top.
Pollen, like a yellow dust,
comes from the tassels.

Why? Eric wonders.

Wind blows the pollen
to the cornsilk
growing from each
little ear of corn.

Yellow kernels,
hidden by
green leaves,
get big
and sweet.

Eric's pumpkins take a long, long time to grow.

He knows pumpkins need more time than carrots, onions, or corn.

There are
bright yellow flowers.

Then at last
there are little green pumpkins
under the big leaves.

In October, the pumpkins are big and ripe
and ready to harvest—

Just in time for Halloween!